I dedicate my book to my grandchildren, George, Grace and Patricia and my nephew, Jacob.

Have you ever felt crummy? Patricia and Grace are sisters, and they felt crummy. They had to stay home and away from their friends because of the coronavirus. Their mother told them that staying home kept them safe. Not being with their pals was even worse than eating spinach, cleaning their room, or picking up toys.

The one thing that made the girls' day better was Pinky, a pretty pink rose, in their backyard. Pinky's soft petals made them think of the fluffy kitten at their Cousin George's house. They so wished they had a pet. Then one day they had a big surprise.

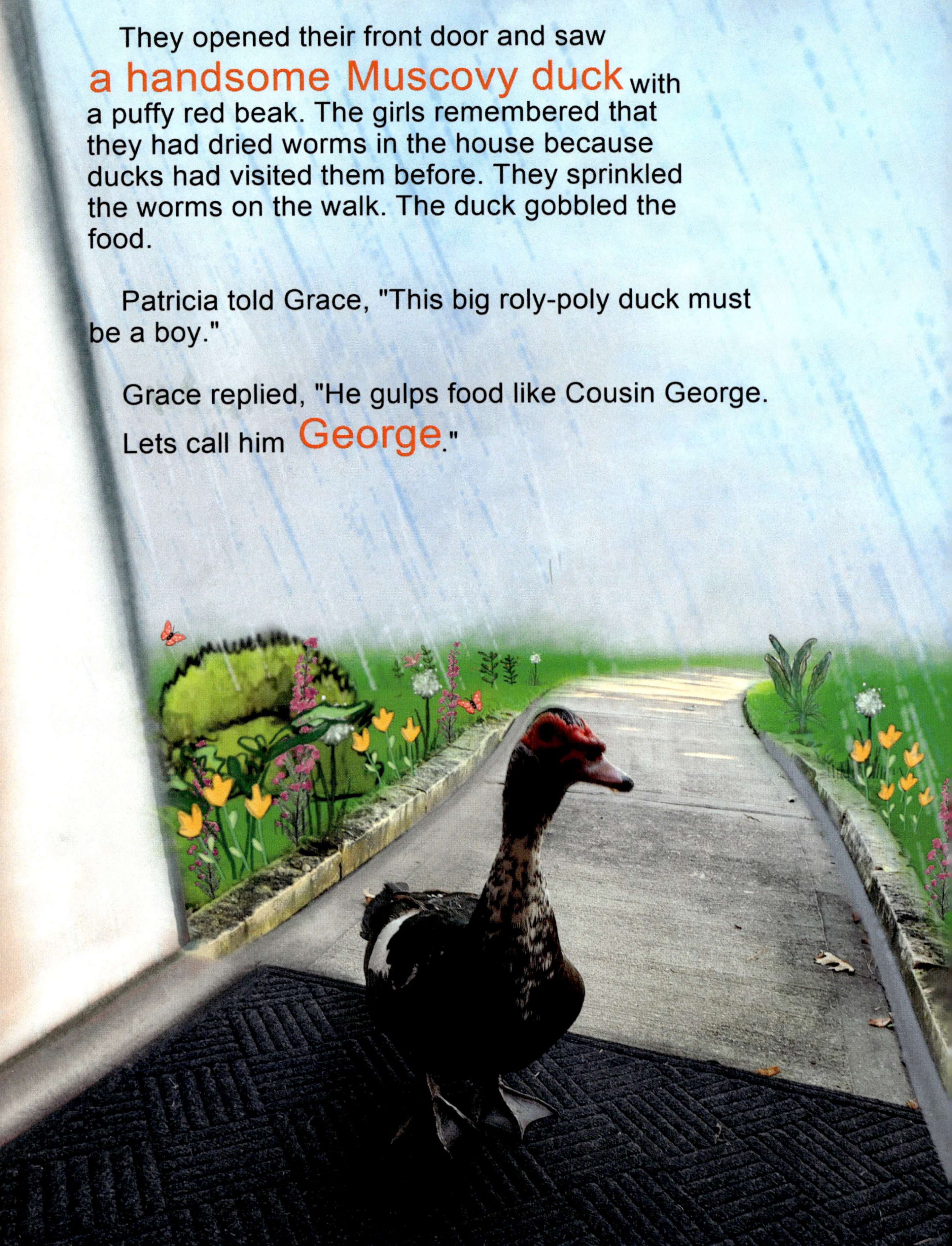

They opened their front door and saw **a handsome Muscovy duck** with a puffy red beak. The girls remembered that they had dried worms in the house because ducks had visited them before. They sprinkled the worms on the walk. The duck gobbled the food.

Patricia told Grace, "This big roly-poly duck must be a boy."

Grace replied, "He gulps food like Cousin George. Lets call him **George**."

Suddenly the girls heard a clap of thunder. George got scared and ran down the street. The girls hurried after him. Then it began to rain. They didn't care about getting wet. They cared about George. They found him hiding safely in some bushes. So, they ran back home. George had made their stay-at-home day so much better.

The next day George came to visit again while the girls were playing outside. He shook his tail feathers and bobbed his head up and down.

Grace had read that Muscovy ducks show friendship with their head and tail feathers.

When the girls sprinkled food on the sidewalk George did something amazing. He ate more than the worms. He snapped at mosquitos and swallowed them, too!

"Wow!" said Grace. "Daddy will love George. He hates mosquito bites."

While George continued eating, the girls went to say hello to Pinky. When they came back to see George, he was no longer there.

Patricia shouted, "This duck is just like Cousin George. Sometimes he is unavailable."

"Yes," Grace said, "when we ask George to help pick up toys, he tells us that he is unavailable."

Grace and Patricia did not see George for another week. When they fed George this time, he did not look at them.

Patricia whispered to Grace, "Maybe George left last time because we went to visit Pinky. He is scared we will disappear again."

Grace and Patricia both patted George on his back.

After George finished eating, he shuffled away wagging his tail feathers and bobbing his head. He was still their friend. He settled on the soft grass under the oak tree looking as happy as a kid at a birthday party. Suddenly, a squirrel jumped from the tree and landed on top of George. He lifted his wings and flew away.

Grace and Patricia's mother had a coronavirus talk with them. She told the girls that they must stand six feet away from others and wear a mask to stop the spread of the virus. So, the next time George visited, they wore their masks and kept their distance. George seemed puzzled and hurried away.

The next day the girls sadly discovered that Pinky was not on the rose bush. Roses only last so long. Then they noticed the jumpy squirrel smelling a yellow rose.

"Lets call this yellow rose Sunshine," Patricia said.

Later they spotted George with a boy down the street. They waved to George, but he turned away.

"Grace, George likes boys better than girls," shouted Patricia.

Grace sadly replied, "Sunshine is our only friend now."

Two days later George was on the girls' front lawn. They put on their masks and ran outside to put some food down for George. He stayed away from them. His visit was not about food for a duck. He wanted Grace and Patricia to know that he was still their friend, even six feet away. Suddenly, he scurried to the other side of the front walk.

George had heard his other friend calling him. The boy was wearing a mask this time. The girls invited the boy to play with them in the backyard. The boy told the girls that his name was Jacob. Grace, Patricia, and Jacob played together all afternoon - six feet apart while George slept under the front yard tree.

The girls thought everything was perfect. They had two new friends. However, the next time George visited, they had another concern.

George was limping. He had injured his foot. Patricia had read that turtles sometimes attack ducks. She wondered if a turtle had bit George's foot. George stood near the flower garden and looked away. He did not want Grace and Patricia to come near him. He just flapped his tail feathers in friendship.

When he left, the girls were worried about George.

To feel better, Grace went inside the house. She put on a pretty apron and decorated some freshly baked cookies.

Patricia stayed outside and drew a crazy chalk picture of herself on the driveway.

When Patricia and Grace spotted George again, he was sniffing flowers in the neighbor's yard. His foot was better.

Patricia yelled, "I wish that I was a duck like George. I could go everywhere."

Grace replied, "George can go everywhere, but he has had tough times, too. A squirrel jumped on him. He hurt his foot. George always finds ways to make himself happy."

George waddled to the flower garden and plucked two flowers with his beak. He put them on the ground six feet from the girls. They picked up the flowers and thanked him. George had made the girls stop feeling sorry for themselves. They decided to think of fun ways to entertain themselves.

Grace painted a picture of Pinky and Sunshine.

Patricia told Grace, "Your picture is pretty, but not as pretty as Pinky and Sunshine."

"Real roses disappear," Grace said, "but a rose picture lasts forever."

Patricia painted a picture of George.

Grace said, "You painted George crazy colors. George is black, brown and green."

"Well, an artist does not have to use real colors," Patricia replied. "I like these colors and thought they would look handsome on George."

The girls had a message for the coronavirus that causes *COVID - 19.* They wrote a poem.

Fun Duck Day Six Feet Away

Until there`s a vaccine,
To cure *COVID – 19,*
With a duck we can play,
Staying six feet away.

Gracious George we adore,
When he waits at our door,
No crummy days anymore,
Lots more fun than before.

Then Patricia and Grace picked up their toys and cleaned their bedrooms. They both liked their super-terrific clean rooms.

For lunch their mom made a spinach salad with strawberries. The salad was yummy. They liked spinach now.

George showed the girls how to turn crummy coronavirus days into chummy fun days. Maybe ducks are smarter than people.

Thank-you George for your wisdom.

Made in the USA
Las Vegas, NV
15 December 2020

13577247R00017